A.   ACKNOWLEDGEMENTS

I would like to dedicate this work to Caliph Ali Ibne Abi Talib (A.S), the Fourth Caliph, and successor of The Prophet Muhammad (PBUH) according to the Shia, the essence of whose life's work was to serve the Ummah of the Prophet Mohamed (PBUH) and preserve its unity. One of his sayings which inspires me and which I would like to share is "Loss is distributed exactly according to the ratio of investment and the profit is distributed according to the agreement of the partners." This is the foundation of the rules of sharing risks and rewards in accordance with Islamic Sharia

I would like acknowledge the support and contributions of my family and friends who influenced, encouraged and supported me in this endeavour. I would like to acknowledge the spiritual contribution of my mother Late Mrs. Shirin Ebrahim, who pushed me to pursue excellence, loved me unconditionally and inspired me to follow the path to actualise my talents and dreams.

I am responsible for anything controversial in the book, is not meant to undermine any school of thought/individual, as its objective is to increase knowledge.

Mohamed Abdulla Ebrahim

November 2019

CHAPTER 1

Introduction to Green Finance and Sustainable Finance and its Connection to SDG's

In recent years, the Sustainable Development Goals (SDG) set by the United Nations (UN) have risen on the top of the development agenda, with an emphasis on a partnership approach between the financed and financier. Given the scale of the financial resources required to support the SDG, coupled with the strain on government budgets, the mobilization of financing through innovative instruments becomes imperative. Islamic finance, through the *Maqasid al-Sharia* – Islamic moral economy values are the foundation for Islamic finance, where participatory modes of investment take centre stage.

Hence, the potential of the use of Islamic finance to support green investments to finance the SDG agenda that has been receiving increased attention.

This is an emerging niche within the Islamic Environmental, Social, Governance financing arena, wherein the recent past issues of a few green *Sukuk* to finance climate friendly projects, water and sanitation projects, clean energy projects. The rise of Ethical Social Governance (ESG) friendly investors and investment managers enhance this trend, who will mobilize the funds for investing in green sustainable projects.

It is in this contextual melting pot of ESG investing, Islamic moral value-based financial products, and impact investing, where innovative participatory finance will fusion to enable funding for green sustainable projects to actualize the SDG.

Islamic modes of finance can be the key to the achievement of the SDG, which will make our world a better place for all its inhabitants. This is because when we make the earth greener, and address the challenge of climate change and building key infrastructure in the least developed countries.

The infrastructure to be developed would be like enabling the provision of clean water and decent sanitation and waste disposal systems, ensuring attainable housing is available, enabling sustainable energy sources like wind and solar, creating opportunities in the blue economy, may result in increasing the livelihood of the world's poorest inhabitants and uplift their living standards. These are goals that are congruent with *Maqasid* al-Sharia. The chapter will discuss how the various concepts of Islamic finance like *Mudharabah*, *Musharakah*, *Istinah*, Salaam, etc. at the micro-level and *Sukuk* (Islamic bond) at the macro level can be used to provide solutions to achieving green and SDG objectives. Hence. More research and product development in this area will be taking place in the next few years.

Robert Schiller, 2013 Nobel Laurate in Economic's in his book "Finance and the Good Society" says

"Finance is not about 'making money' per se. It is a 'functional' science in that it exists to support other goals – those of the society.

The better aligned a society's financial institutions are with its goals and ideals, the stronger and more successful the society will be." (Shiller, 2012: 7)

Finance "is not, and should not be, merely a zero-sum game, but rather an adjunct to, and a means toward a productive life." (Shiller, 2012: 104)

CHAPTER 2:

The Need for Green solutions, where SDG's and Islamic Moral Finance Principles meet

Our planet has the following challenges which are becoming critical to its sustainability: -

1) Global warming and climate change.

2) Huge disparities between the capital and infrastructure development between the developed world and the developing world.

3) Extreme poverty in developing countries.

These challenges were initially intended
to be addressed by the UN's Millennium
Development Goals, set in the run-up to
the year 2000, which however failed to
make a major impact to the lives of
world's poorest inhabitants,
subsequently, these were reformulated
and expanded and articulated as
Sustainable Development Goals (SDG)
by the United Nations.

Islamic finance, with its philosophical roots in Islamic Moral economy values, developed in the golden age of Islamic Caliphate by scholars like *Ibn Khaldun*, in this period is gaining wider acceptance and growing fast among scholars and practitioners. This economic philosophy promotes the sharing of risk and returns between the financed and financiers, and participatory finance as it is termed in Turkey is regaining lost ground. It was time that the goal congruence of SDG and Islamic values are realized and adopted by the global financial community.

This is where Green Sustainable finance using *Sukuk* (Islamic Bond) at the macro level and the other modes like Salaam, *Istisnah, Musharaka*, and *Mudharabah,* at the micro-level come into fusion to provide finance for green sustainable projects and businesses.

The Sustainable Development goals where these can be applied are as described below:-

Food Security for Nations and Sustainable Agriculture

One of the biggest challenges of the developing world especially Africa, parts of Asia and Latin America, is ensuring that droughts do not cause deaths due to lack of availability of decent quantities and nutritionally proper nutritional types for local populations in a cost-effective way, consistently throughout the year and proper to meet basic human needs. The measures would include sustainable agricultural methods and food crops and domesticated animals. These sustenance crops grown and livestock reared, should be after harvest, be stored in a manner that can last till the next harvest. It should be ensured the acreage is used optimally, the domesticated animals reared and a crop is grown currently should be capable of serving the needs of future generations of humankind.

To ensure this food security, potentially could involve issuing green *Sukuk's* for large scale commercial farming and farmed forests, from which wood would be harvested and also designed in a manner to retain the eco-system of the water-catchment area's.

Furthermore, Salaam, which was initially developed to finance agricultural activities, could be revived in the modern context to finance the small scale farmer in rural areas.

Health

The delivery of dependable, access to cost-effective, and superior health-related services, professional medical advice and medication to the people effectively and efficiently, and meeting their requirements, and suitable for their particular environment. This would also involve how healthcare is going to be financed, like social insurance for health care; this would be where the concept of health takaful would be appropriate.

Renewable and clean power

The creation and usage of maintainable power sources for businesses, people, and cities, to satisfy the requirements of the currently living people without compromising the capacity of future generations to satisfy their future power needs. The renewable power sources would include wind, hydro, geothermal, and solar energy sources that could be harnessed. Power generating and distribution corporations and real estate developers should be encouraged to invest in solar, and wind projects, by issuing Green *Sukuk's* for such projects.

Sanitation and Water

The supply of sanitation and water and services of adequate quality and quantity to meet baseline standards of living. This would include access to water for meeting basic needs. National and sub-national governments could issue Green *Sukuk* to finance water desalination plants and distribute water, which is treated and safe to its citizens. It could take the form of Public-Private partnerships.

Housing

The availability of attainable, permanent housing of a suitable standard and condition to house people in a cost-effective manner. Housing is extremely circumstantial based on materials available locally, climate, and geography. *Ijarah* and diminishing *Musharakah* could be used to finance housing, and *istisnah* could be used to develop housing projects.

Education

The availability of inexpensive, reliable, and excellent education to school-going children in a manner relevant to the native contexts. Practically it means the supply of at least free elementary education for both girls and boys. Islamic *qardan hassanah* (interest-free loan) and *Zakat* (mandatory charitable alms on qualifying persons) funds could be utilized in the educational context, and Sukuk *Ijara* could be issued for building educational establishments.

Financial Services

Enable financial inclusion in the economy that is suitable for the pay scale of the individual and requirements of the lender to develop financial empowerment and inspire involvement in the formal and informal segments by using consumers and small business products and services. Islamic *Sharia* Compliant, microfinance services, including credit unions and savings and credit co-operative, could address this inclusivity gap. **Mahmoud Mohieldin (2017),**

Sustainable development Goals and Islamic Finance

It is estimated that the hole in funding available to meet SDGs in developing countries is projected at US$ 2.5 trillion annually; this is significantly beyond the capacity of any individual government or development agency. Hence, it will require a wider coalition of associates, fresh activists, and fresh outlooks, especially those from the commercial finance side, to conjointly advance growth efforts. These agencies place importance on all-inclusiveness and wide appreciation of commercial and communal dynamics, Islamic finance values remain extremely synchronized to the SDG, therefore creating new partnerships in this domain will be critical and easy, to supply the much-desired boost to implement the SDG 2030 Agenda, using finance as a catalyst. Sekretar A. (2017),

An instance of the robust partnership that connects Islamic finance with the SDGs is the Global Islamic Finance and Impact Investing Platform (GIFIIP), which was created by the United Nations Development Program in partnership with Islamic Development Bank in September 2015. This platform enables the provision of market-based answers to growth challenges and aims at positioning Islamic impact investing as an enabler of SDG implementation.

CHAPTER 3:

The Green Islamic Finance Impact Investing Program (GIFIIP)

Objectives and anticipated outcomes of the GIFIIP:

1. United Nations Development Program (UNDP) and the Islamic Development Bank's (IDB), research and training arm Islamic Research and Training Institute (IRTI) jointly commissioned a study, "I for Impact: Blending Islamic Finance and Impact Investing for the Global Goals," in 2017. The study enunciates the parallels and concerted effort amongst Islamic finance and impact investing hence building an empowering business-case among the network of investing and finance for the SDGs. GIFIIP has

also established the Islamic finance and impact investing training program to assist players in the Islamic finance niche to build their capabilities to take hold of SDG financing prospects. This platform was launched in Pakistan in August 2016 and is intended to be simulated in Muslim majority nations and member nations of the Organisation of Islamic Countries (OIC).

2. It is envisioned that through this platform, the UNDP will approve the arrangement for Islamic commercial investment and finance to recommend qualifying Islamic *sharia*-compliant

investments that are in sync with the SDGs. This agreement would be affected by the Islamic Finance Council UK and Islamic Research and Training Institute, the training arm of Islamic Development Bank, and including the associates of the sustainable development goals Impact platform. This move would enable private sector players, and Islamic financiers, Islamic investment managers, and investors to ascertain investable opportunities whilst benchmarking the factual influence of their involvement with the sustainable development goals agenda outcomes.

3. Realize the hidden possibilities of green Sukuk to finance sustainable development goal projects and initiatives, GIFIIP rolled out a fresh set of Green Sukuk investor training to create an increased recognition of the model and the prospective impact in the renewable power sector with regard to Islamic investors. Green Sukuk is a distinctive illustration of Islamic *sharia* created impact investing security that shows how resources mobilized from Islamic *sharia* conscious investors could be used towards renewable power projects. The world's debut Green Sukuk was listed in Malaysia to finance a solar

energies); -components of the financial system that deal specifically with green investments, such as the Green Climate Fund or financial instruments for green investments (e.g. green bonds and structured green funds), including their specific legal, economic and institutional framework conditions"

Höhne, Khosla, Fekete, and Gilbert (2012) assert that green finance initiatives products and are projects that aim towards sustainable development.

Green Islamic finance, would mean all of the above if they comply with Islamic values and principles.

Islamic Impact Investing

The phrase "Islamic impact investing" provokes numerous reactions ranging from jubilation to misperception to contempt, some say this is just misuse of the word Islamic, to get funds from the Petrodollar rich Gulf Countries. As with the development of the more developed financial-market for Social Responsible Investing (SRI) which started around 25 years ago, Islamic *sharia* compliant impact investing phenomena is the newest frontline that exceeds the limitations of negative screening methodologies, and actively seeks affirmative intent in investments that adhere to Islamic sharia principles and which provides both positive returns financially and measurable impact on the social indicators (SI's).

Islamic Impact investments are defined as those Islamic sharia-compliant investments made into collective investment funds like unit trust and mutual funds, corporates and private companies, national and sub-national government units, private-public partnership projects, which in their charter documents like investment policy statements, vision and strategy statements have the objective to generate social and environmental impact alongside a financial return.

JP Morgan Chase looks a wider definition of Impact investments, in the traditional finance arena as Impact investments are those investments intended to create a positive impact beyond financial return. As such, they require the active management and measurement of social indicators (SI's) and environmental impact indicators (EII's), in addition to financial risk and return rates.

The Global Impact Investing Network (GIIN), additionally enlarges the features of impact investing in comprising the following:

- Intentionality – The intention of the financier is to produce social and environmental impact via the Investment selection process, and the screening procedure is a critical constituent of impact investing.

- Return expectations of Investments – Impact investments are projected to produce a positive financial return on the investment and, at least, a return of the principal amount invested.

- Range of asset classes with tied return expectations – Impact investments are expected to produce returns that vary from less than the market (concessionary term return) to risk-adjusted market-rate returns.

- Impact measurement – A symbol of impact investing is the obligation of the investor to the quantity and provide a statement on the environmental and social parameters achieved and the development of the underlying investments.

Impact measurement assists in ensuring transparent and accountable systems and processes that are critical to notifying the stakeholders of the exercise of impact investing and structuring the investment.

These would normally include reporting on key performance indicators related to the objective like acreage covered with trees, reducing x units of carbon emissions in a given period.

Tegegnework Gettu, (2018)

CHAPTER 4:

Principles of Islamic Finance embedded in Green Finance

Basis of Islamic sharia principles in Green Islamic Finance.

Qu'ranic and *hadith* related values drive the Islamic investment and financing niche. A majority of people mistake that Islamic investing relates to the fact that interest (*Riba*) is not given or taken, and some people frequently believe in the fallacious notion that Islamic financial contracts are a disguise for charging "interest" using a different name, like rent or profit. In reality, Islamic investing is driven by several basic tenets and economic philosophies. This "Islamic Sharia-compliance" aspect is supervised by scholars conversant with Islamic commercial jurisprudence *"fiqh mualmat"* as Sharia Boards or committees.

Sharia Principles

According to numerous regular finance experts and investors, Islamic *Sharia-* compliant financing and investing is tantamount to applying the restraining elucidations of the *Qur'an*.

Once this is focused on the investing and financial sector, Islamic sharia compliance results in the way of arranging finance-related dealings in a way that cash has no inherent value, and the dealings promote a huge communal good through linking returns with risk-sharing.

Therefore, these are not constraining rules but a social charter that is different from traditionally designed financial services. The fundamental doctrines of *Sharia* values are stated below:-

• **Interest** is forbidden. Interest is referred to an increase in the principal sum without any sharing of risks of the venture or transaction and the increase in the principal sum by the mere passage of time, i.e., the time value of money concept does not hold in Islamic finance. Interest is forbidden on both sides of the deal i.e., paying and receiving.

• **Game of Chance, Uncertainity and Pure Speculation** (*Maisir* and *Gharar*) is proscribed. Activities which are included are gambling, pure speculation, hedging as a profit centre, or any transaction or agreement which includes an element of chance or excessive uncertainty.

- **Forbidden (*Haram*)** business activities or industrial activities. Some of these are specifically prohibited in the Quran and other based on hadiths on causing harm. Illustrations include businesses that earn a substantial amount of income (higher than 5%) from the sale or distribution of intoxicants, tobacco, pork, weapons manufacturing, gambling, pornography, and financial firms that earn interest or give interest.

AAOIFI guiding principles to screen financing and investment opportunities state that if the balance sheet and profit and loss account of a company have the following characteristics, then these should not be invested in:-

1) Businesses with leverage (debt to equity) greater than 30%,

2) Companies with debtors (receivables) ratio to total assets are more than 45%, or

3) Businesses with income derived from interest are higher than 5%, or interest expense is more than 5% of expenses.

Risk should be borne by both parties, institutions, and investors.

Investors are those parties who provide the funding. They are not creditors in their traditional sense that are certain or expect a certain rate of return; this is measured by profit share, fees, or any other form of compensation. The institution is a manager of a venture, who share the risk of the project, transaction or deal with the investors; those risks are pooled by mutual sharing of consequences of a negative event and the distribution of profits or losses, to both the parties.

Cash has no intrinsic worth.

Cash on its own has value, hence cannot it is not a commodity of worth to be bought or sold. **Cash** growth or declines in worth only occurs when used with other assets for constructive activities, as a measure of value and medium of exchange. **Cash**, unless fused together with other assets, cannot grow in value over time; growth in value cannot be derived simply due to the passage time, based on amount. All transactions should be based on active, economically productive work. Investments must be made in physical, tangible, assets that generate income, directly or indirectly, and real physical or tangible assets must also back transactions related to securitization.

Contractual terms should be clear

Terms and conditions of contracts should be clear relating to terms of contributions of capital and efforts, including expectations of all parties concerning sharing both the profit and loss. All parties must have an awareness of the tangible products or services being transacted as they are agents for each other and the transactional values. Agreements must be mutually agreed to by all parties and should be for a defined period of time or stated at the onset that they are perpetual, with clearly defined mechanisms for future changes.

Zakat (Obligatory Charitable giving)

A *Qu'ranic* principle that is unique in Islamic financing and investing is the principle of *zakat* or mandatory giving usually based on 2.5% of wealth, above a certain level, to the eight specified categories of persons, in the Quran, plus to those to whom its should not be given, like one's own family and descendants of the Prophet Muhammad (PBUH).

This is meant to be an active response to helping those in need. Islamic investment managers sometimes, provide mechanisms for payment of *Zakat* on the investment income for their clients, who adhere to the Islamic faith.

Hence, a *Zakat* fund account is maintained by many Islamic Financial Institutions, detailing the collection and distribution of the *Zakat* collected

Sadaqah and Cleansing

The **cleansing** doctrine necessitates that any investment return that maybe unclean based on Islamic commercial jurisprudence rules, should be given to charity if it may have been generated from activities defined as unlawful according to. This rule covers all types of investors and investments. As we cannot at all times be sure of the source of the incomes of clients and or investee units, Islamic Financial Institutions should according to their own judgement give a fixed percentage (say 5% to 10%) of their income as a voluntary charitable contribution in form of institutional *sadaqah*, through their *sadaqah* account.

Furthermore, when a party transacting with an Islamic financial institution defaulting on its obligations, and a contractual penalty is payable, this will also go to the *sadaqah* account.

Azzad Funds, based in the US, even has a **cleansing** calculator on its website for real-time calculation of the calculated amount for **cleansing** and to provide guidance for *Sadaqah* payment (a voluntary contribution to charity).

It should be understood that the *sadaqah,* may not always make the unclean income clean, but it will increase the reward (*Thawab*) so as to make the wrongdoing comparatively negligible.

The *sadaqah* funds can be used in any charitable activity and have fewer restrictions as to the parties to whom this can be distributed; therefore social impact investments may be funded therefrom, like building schools, medical centre, etc.

CHAPTER 5:

Conceptual structures of Islamic Finance

Key Structures for Green Islamic financing

An assortment of structures for Sharia-compliant financing and investing activities exist, however, the emphasis will be in types of Islamic finance deemed most appropriate for Islamic impact investing and widely used currently in Islamic financing and investment sphere namely: Sukuk (Financial Certificate), *Musharaka* (Partnership), *Murabaha* (cost-plus financing), *Istisna* (build/manufacture/construct financing), and *Ijarah* (lease).

It is noteworthy, *Qard-e-Hasssnah*, will not be considered since it is mostly a compassionate loan and hence considered as a form of aid, not an investment.

Although, It has been observed in practice that some microfinance institutions are building business models around the *Qard-e-Hasnah* concept, on rotating group savings, with group members guaranteeing each other, with administrative fees charged to cover costs, but it is yet to be determined, whether or not these transactions are transferable geographically, profitable, scalable, and sustainable in the long run. These are mostly based on the model pioneered in Bangladesh by *Grameen Bank*. Despite these schemes having potential as a valuable tool for financial inclusion, these are usually set up as saving and credit societies or credit unions.

Sukuk

Sukuk is a document of title (security) related to specific assets or asset classes underpinning it. *Sukuk* are not without dispute as some scholars and individual feel that the time value of money and the making of money above the sum initially advanced, from it, is in-built, in the long term nature of a market tradeable Sukuk. In a *Sukuk* transaction, the borrower sells the certificates of ownership of the assists or group of assets, similar to a collateralized debt obligation (CBO) to a group of investors.

The investor rents the asset back to the borrower and earns income rent or profit based on a predetermined rental charge or profit rate. The borrower undertakes a commitment to buy back the asset underpinning the certificate, of the contractual instrument, on a specified date at face value. If listed on a securities exchange, the value in the intermittent period fluctuates based on market conditions, hence the possibility of earning a profit on the sale of the security.

Sukuk can have a variety of underlying assets defined as a right to receive future streams of income or usage benefits, from which income streams can be derived. In effect, ownership of a Sukuk is partial ownership in debt (*Murabaha*), asset (*Ijarah*), project (*Istisna*), business (*Musharaka*) or investment (*mudharaba*) contractual structures. If the underlying assets transferred and contracts are diligently prepared in accordance with the rules governing them by the lawyers and approved by a credible *Sharia* board, the concerns of the paragraph above will have been addressed.

The debut sovereign nation to sell and promote a *Sukuk* was The Kingdom of Bahrain in the year 2001, which opened the gates for sovereign nations selling *Sukuk*. As of July 2014, *Sukuk* amounts outstanding were approximately $296B, with sovereign nation sellers accounting for 36% of the total market. The in a year biggest sellers corporates and the Malaysian Sovereign and Sub- Sovereign *Sukuk* sellers. In June of 2014, the United Kingdom became the first western country to sell a sovereign *Sukuk*; this was significantly oversubscribed, receiving buy orders of £2.3 billion having been placed on the issuance of £200m ($322m). Between the years 2002 to 2012, annual *Sukuk* sold grew at an average rate of 35%, from $4 billion to $83 billion. Although the majority of *Sukuk* are

Intended for home country financial markets (and issued in local currency), international EuroDollar *Sukuk* sold is growing from 10% in 2010 to 20% in 2014 of the sovereign *Sukuk* market.

There is a need and potential for a forestry-based Green *Sukuk*, would in purchasing large parcels of land say in Africa and or the Australian interior, which would be planted with native trees and managed as a sustainable rainforest. This rainforest would be a catchment area for rainfall and also reduce CO_2 emissions. It would earn revenue through the sale of Carbon credits and also the timber, grown as a managed agri-forest.

Other uses would be wind farms, solar
power farms, dams on rivers, hospitals,
and health care facilities, schools in
Africa, Asia, South America, etc.

Murabaha

Murabaha is the favourite Islamic Sharia-
compliant contract used by Islamic
Financial Institutions. It is a trade-based
structure usually used for short-term
financing needs, mainly to inventory
needed as working capital, set up as a
sale contract, where the inventory is
bought by the Islamic Financial

Institution and sold with a mark-up to the client, payable in instalments. It is also used by the sovereign nation to issue treasury *Sukuk* for short-term borrowing. The underlying item is owned by the Islamic Financial Institution until the buyer completes the payments.

Ijarah

An *Ijarah* is a lease contract mainly used for financing of, motor vehicles, equipment financing, plant, and machinery, or home finance, with a fixed period of time, with the regular periodic flow of payments. Legal ownership of the asset remains with the financier until the payment schedule of the contract has been fulfilled. Lease payments are agreed to be in advance over a specific time period.

A *Sukuk Ijara* is ideal for long term financing of projects like wind farms, solar projects, hospital complexes, school complexes, where the project is built on behalf of the operator (using *Istisna*), is bought from the proceeds of the *Sukuk* issue, and asset leased back to the operator who makes the periodic payments generated by the usage of the product or service, e.g., sale of electricity, rental of the healthcare facility, rental of school facility, etc.

Istisna

Istisna is a contract to construct, make, or build a specialized item or asset for an end purchaser. Mainly used as project finance to finance long term, large scale facilities like manufacturing plants, housing projects, solar power plants, airports, bridges, roads, and natural resource mining operations. It is a tripartite agreement between financier, end purchaser, and builder, manufacturer or contractor. A contractor, get a contract to build an asset, from the end-user, they approach an Islamic Financial Institution, who finances the build stage, once built they sell it to the Islamic Financial Institution, who then sell it to the end-user. The end-user can further, have it refinanced for the long term using the Sukuk contract structure.

Musharaka and *Mudaraba*

Musharaka and *Mudaraba's* contracts being equity-based contractual arrangements include profit and loss sharing and risk sharing, hence have no controversy among Sharia scholars.

Musharaka is a joint owned asset arrangement (like diminishing *musharaka* for home financing) or venture formed for the purpose of equity participation. The participants provide capital in accordance with pre-agreed ration and share the profits in accordance with a pre-agreed ratio, however losses according to capital contribution ratio.

Mudaraba is a partnership in which several non-active investor partners (*Arbab Al Maal*) gives money to the investment or venture managing partner (*mudrib*) for the financing of a commercial venture or investment portfolio. The managing partner (*mudrib*), received a percentage of profits for his efforts to manage the venture, but not share in the loss, and is not entitled to any other compensation. If the *Mudaraba* agreement allows the *Mudrib*, it can also contribute to the capital of the venture, for which he will be treated like any other investor partner; however, he will still be compensated with a separate profit share, for his management efforts. Profits are shared in accordance with the pre-agreed ratio between the *Mudrib* and *Arbaab al Maal*, whereas financial losses are borne entirely by the investor partners. The *Arbaab al Maal's* will share their profit allocation in accordance with their capital contribution ratios. This is very similar to the practices of traditional venture capital funds.

Hence potential, products to be developed could by projects in farming food crops, fishing and rearing of livestock, storing them ensuring minimal damage and wastage, and agricultural processing and distribution of the same based on community-based youth groups organized as *musharaka* or *mudharaba* (if there is a financing partner involved) concepts.

CHAPTER 6:

Simplified Case Studies

Case Study 1 – First Corporate Green *Sukuk* by Majid Al Futtaim Group

On the 15th May 2019, Majid Al Futtaim group of companies created history, by listing on NASDAQ stock exchange Dubai, the world's debut Green Sukuk issued by a corporate entity for USD 600 million to finance its positive environmental impact strategy and back the conversion to a low-carbon economy in Dubai, United Arab Emirates.

Company Background

Majid Al Futtaim (the "Issuer," the "Company," or "MAF") is an owner, operator, and developer of retail and commercial properties in the Middle Eastern & North African (MENA) region. Established in 1992, MAF operates 40, shopping malls, hotels, and multiple-use developments, with other projects underway, through its three active firms namely: Majid Al Futtaim Properties, Majid Al Futtaim Retail, and Majid Al Futtaim Ventures, it has developed the Majid Al Futtaim Green Finance Framework (the "Framework") through which it intends to sell a series of green bonds and/or green *Sukuk* and use the capital funds raised to finance and refinance, wholly or partly, currently existing and future projects that will provide environmentally positive impact and support the transition to a low-carbon economy. According to the Framework, the qualifying criteria fall under four areas:

1. Green Buildings
2. Renewable Energy
3. Sustainable Water Management
4. Energy Efficiency

2nd Opinion by Sustainalytics - Sustainability report

Opinion

"Sustainalytics is of the opinion that the Majid Al Futtaim Green Finance Framework is credible and impactful, and aligns with the four core components of the Green Bond Principles 2018. Sustainalytics highlights the following elements of Majid Al Futtaim's Framework:

Use of Proceeds: The four eligible project categories

Ø green buildings,

Ø renewable energy,

Ø sustainable water management,

Ø energy efficiency

The use of the proceed from the Green
  bonds, or Green Sukuk are in alignment
  with those acknowledged as impactful by
  the Green Bond Principles 2018 and
  Sustainalytics is of the opinion that
  investments under Majid Al Futtaim's
  Framework will deliver positive
  environmental outcomes.

Majid Al Futtaim uses credible third-party
  certifications for its green building
  eligibility criteria, namely BREEAM (Very
  Good and above) and LEED (Gold and

above). Sustainalytics considers the selected certification schemes to be robust and credible, and the selected minimum certification levels to deliver positive impacts. Sustainalytics further encourages MAF to certify to the level of BREEAM Excellent where possible.

Eligible technologies for renewable energy are defined as wind and solar power; Sustainalytics considers these energy sources to have positive overall environmental impacts. Sustainalytics notes that these investments include both capital expenditures, as well as the procurement of renewable energy from other producers. To ensure additionality and strong impact, Sustainalytics encourages MAF to ensure that its renewable energy procurement is, where possible, subject to long-term power purchase agreements (PPAs) that support the construction of energy projects.

Sustainalytics views positively that, within the categories of sustainable water management and energy efficiency, MAF has established quantitative thresholds for eligibility. Limiting eligible projects to those that lead to 30% improvements in water use and 20% improvements in energy use will ensure that the projects financed by the Framework provide high levels of impact.

Project Evaluation and Selection:

The Project Selection and Evaluation Process will be managed by Majid Al Futtaim's Green Finance Steering Committee, consisting of members of the Company's Sustainability Committee and a member of the Treasury team. The committee will be chaired by the Treasurer and will, on an annual basis, select new eligible projects for Inclusion in the Portfolio, replace any projects in the Portfolio that are no longer eligible, and implement any necessary Framework updates.

Proceeds Management:

Majid Al Futtaim shall deposit the net proceeds of each green bond or green *Sukuk*, in the Company's general funding accounts, where they will be earmarked for allocation using a Green Finance Register, containing information regarding each green bond and green Sukuk. Proceeds not yet allocated will be invested in accordance with the Company's liquidity policy.

Sustainalytics notes that MAF will value assets in its Portfolio at book value in line with accounting standards. This approach will ensure that assets are appropriately represented in the portfolio of projects despite the lack of a formal lookback period.

Based on the use of a green finance register, and the disclosure of assets under construction, Sustainalytics considers MAF's management of proceeds to be in line with market practice.

Reporting:

Majid Al Futtaim commits to publishing an annual allocation report and impact report regarding its Green Eligible Project Portfolio. The allocation report will contain a list of Eligible Projects, the total amount allocated to each Eligible Project, the amount by Project Category, and the balance of unallocated proceeds. This process is in line with current market practice, and Sustainalytics highlights, in particular, the highly granular level of reporting.

Majid Al Futtaim's impact report will be provided at the level of each Project Category and may include relevant metrics such as level of certification by the property, estimated GHG emissions avoided, amount of water recycled and expected energy saved. This process is in line with market standards.

" . (**Sustainalytics Report, 2019**)

Simplified Case Study 2 – Malaysia Quasi Sovereign Green Sukuk

Background

Malaysia has the third-largest capital market in Asia and a leading Islamic finance hub. Following the emergence of issuance of Green Bond to tackle climate change challenges, in early 2017, the World Bank, Bank Negara the central bank of Malaysia, and Securities Commission Malaysia, established a technical working group to explore options for developing a green Islamic finance market in Malaysia and for encouraging investments in green or sustainable projects. This technical working group came up with the concept of the "green Sukuk" and tried to sell the idea of a green Sukuk based on green bond issuance with the Ministry of Energy, Green Technology and Water (KeTTHA), Green Tech Malaysia Sdn Bhd, Ministry of Finance, Malaysian financial institutions, and other potential issuers.

Results

Tadau Energy a Malaysian quasi-sovereign entity, in July 2017, issued the first green Sukuk in the world, raising

RM 250 million (US$59 million) to finance a 50 MW power plant in Sabah, Malaysia. The Sukuk was issued under Malaysia's SRI Sukuk framework and endorsed by the Shariah Advisory Council; it also benefited from an independent review by the Center for International Climate and Environmental Research Oslo (CICERO). Following this example, Quantum Solar, sold a RM 1 billion (USD 226) million Green Sukuk, for the biggest to date solar power project in South-East Asia with the solar plant having an aggregate capacity of 150MW (AC), or 197MW during peak period. Both these solar power plants are connected to the electricity grid, with guaranteed purchase of the units of electricity produced, enabling payments of the cash flow to the Sukuk investors. Both these issues were primarily local market issues, listed on Kuala Lampur Exchange

Simplified Case Study 3 – Indonesia Sovereign Green Sukuk US$ 1.25 billion

Indonesia is the most populous Muslim majority country, in line with Islamic values of Maslah of the people, it sought to reduce its GHG emissions, following its neighbor Malaysia also decided to issue its green bond for this purpose, based on the sharia principles, hence the issuance by Indonesia of the first Sovereign Green Sukuk in the world. The Sukuk issue was guided by the Green Bond and Green Sukuk Framework and reviewed by an international independent reviewer CICERO.

The proceeds of $1.25bn Green Sukuk were to be invested in selected 'eligible green projects' based on the Green Bond and Green Sukuk Framework. The investor's geographic distribution was 32% Organisation of Islamic countries (OIC) market, 25% Asia, 15% EU, 18% the USA and 10% Indonesia. This proves the global appeal of the issuance of a Green *Sukuk*.

Case Study 4 –

Hazina Development Trust Limited –

An Islamic Microfinance Institution

based in Mombasa, Kenya

Hazina Development Trust Limited, an Islamic sharia inspired Microfinance institution (MFI) based in Kenya, has recently partnered with M-PAYG, to provide finance for its Solar System, which assists in electrification in rural areas of Kenya's Coast-based region. The process works as follows; the Islamic MFI keeps demo units of the solar systems in its offices. If a customer wants to purchase, then it purchases from M-PAYG and sells it on a Cost Plus basis to the customer on an instalment basis over 24 months. It also has an arrangement with a Community based Youth group who make local energy efferent stoves called *Jiko*'s using firewood or charcoal, which are slightly more expensive for the local population, does a *Murabaha* based contract on instalment based payment. In both these instances, the objectives of green and sustainable projects are achieved at a micro=level, directly affecting people, in congruence with *Maqasaid al-Sharia* and *Maslah* objectives of the philosophical foundations of Islamic economics.

CHAPTER 7:

Future Trends and Conclusion

Islamic finance's *Maqasaid Al-Sharia* and sustainable development goals are reaching goal congruence; the challenge is in developing Islamic Sharia-compliant investment vehicles to mobilize the funds.

This would also include creation of Islamic *Sharia* Compliant products and Services whereby Sustainability, Impact investing, and SDG goals can be met. Green *Sukuk* funds, Climate change *Sukuk* funds, Green *Mudharaba* based controlled forestry projects, Green *Musharaka* based reforestation of the middle east and Green *Istisna* projects in which dams will be made to provide water for irrigation, will come of age in the next few years, especially in Africa, South America, and Asia. It is also hoped that more corporate groups will issue green Sukuk in the near future, to ensure we have a sustainable shared future on planet earth. This is a challenge for all players like Islamic fund managers, trustees of wealth, scientists, entrepreneur's, corporate titans, political actors and *sharia* scholars to make this vision of shared prosperity can come true, by academically inclined practitioners to come up with more research, commercial application of the research leading to innovative development of products and services in this area.

Bibliography

Höhne, N., Khosla, S., Fekete, H., & Gilbert, A. (2012). Mapping of green finance delivered by IDFC members in 2011. Cologne: Ecofys. Retrieved from http://www. Idfc .

Lindenberg, N. (2014). Definition of Green Finance. DIE mimeo, 2014. Retrieved from

Mahmoud Mohieldin (2017), Islamic Finance, SDG'S and Impact Investing, a paper presented by, at the Durham Islamic Finance Summer School, 2017.

Sekretar A. (2017), Green Finance and Islamic Finance, International journal of social sciences and educational studies.

Sustainalytics, (2018), Second-Party Opinion Majid Al Futtaim Green Finance Framework

Shiller, Robert, (2012), Finance and the Good Society

Tegegnework Gettu, Speech September 27, 2018, UNDP Associate Administrator: Achieving the SDGs: Potential of Islamic Finance through Innovative investors and instruments

About the Author: CPA Mohamed Ebrahim

Currently he is an Audit Partner in Ace Associates –Certified Public Accountants & CEO Ace Financial Advisory Limited. He holds an MBA from **The University of Manchester (UK)** and has worked for over 20 years with firms in Kenya -Ernst & Young – Assurance Advisory Business Service & Tax Service lines, PKF Kenya Audit Senior, and Devani –Devani & Co. United Arab Emirates -Group Financial Controller - Credo Investments FZE. Canada, McTavish & Co. He served on the ICPAK Coast Branch, Executive Council as Secretary and CPD Convener (2013-15) and from May 2016 to May 2018. Vice – Chair May 2018 to date. He was **commended by ICPAK** in June 2015 for his services to the Accounting profession by ICPAK.

Educational & Professional details

Bachelor of Arts (Hons) – Sustainable Performance Management
Manchester Metropolitan University

Master of Business Administration
The University of Manchester – Manchester Business School

CIFE and Adv. Certified Islamic Finance Executive in Islamic Accounting
Ethica Institute of Islamic Finance, Dubai, UAE.

ACMA,CGMA, Member, Chartered Institute of Management Accountants and Association of International Certified Professional Accountants, registered as a CIMA Member in Practice.

CPA, Practicing member

Institute of Certified Public Accountants of Kenya

FFA/FIPA – Fellow of the Institute of Financial Accountants and Fellow Institute of Public Accountants of Australia

MCSI: Member, Chartered Institute of Securities & Investments

Current Academic studies, a Doctoral Student at the Edinburgh Business School, completed Academic stage, working on doctoral thesis.

www.ingramcontent.com/pod-product-compliance
Lightning Source LLC
Chambersburg PA
CBHW070611220526
45467CB00003B/1377